DRAWING A BLANK
Laura J Booker

Drawing A Blank Copyright Laura J. Booker
Publishing rights Completely Different Publishing

Laura J. Booker has asserted her rights under the Copyright Designs and Patents Act 1988 to be identified as the author of this work. This book is sold subject to the condition that it shall not, by way of trade or otherwise, be lent, resold, hired out, or otherwise circulated without the publisher's prior consent in any form of binding or cover other than that in which it is published and without a similar condition, being imposed on the subsequent purchaser.
This is a work of fiction and any resemblance of the fictional characters to real persons is purely coincidental and non-intentional.

PAPERBACK
ISBN: ISBN: 9798353162681

Author Laura J Booker

Table of Contents

A WORD FROM THE PUBLISHER 7
SICKY 8
FLEA IN MY TIGHTS 10
DRIVING 11
E BAY 13
TERRIBLE TEMPTRESS..14
BORED 16
VEGAN SWEETS...18
WIN THE LOTTO 19
POSTIE PETE 21
PARTY FOX VERSUS THE FERAL CATS..22
BLOW UP DOLL 24
OFFER 26
I'VE KILLED MY CACTUS..27
STUCK 28
GREEDY CAT 29
MISTRESS K..31
BILLY 33
CHIPPY NIGHT 35
CULT...37
DUNGEON 38
BATTLE OF THE HEATING 39
12 DAYS OF CHRISTMAS 41
BARBARA SCARBOROUGH 43
BALLS TO CHRISTMAS 44
HANGOVER..45
TWAS THE FORTNIGHT BEFORE CHRISTMAS 47
SHIT DAY..49
SALES 50
GETTING READY 52
POEM...54
BOXING DAY...55
CHRISTMAS EVE 57
LITTLE BOY...59
STICKY END..61

HOBBIES	63
A NEW HOBBY	64
RUN.	66
WHEN YOU'RE OLD	67
MONEY	69
RAGE	70
GOD OF POO	74
MUCKY BILL THE BUTCHER	76
ANAL	77
CREATURE	79
TOILET	81
FLASHER	82
ONLY GRANS	83
OUCH	85
ALIEN ABDUCTION	86
MADAME TRACKSUIT	88
CAT EXPLOSION	90
TREVOR	91
SKINNY STEVE	92
VIKINGS	93
BEAUTY NIGHT	94
ROGER THE CHICKEN	96
DOG POO	98
ALEXA	99
VALENTINE	100
PENI.	101
OLD.	102
NORMAN THE SEAGULL	103
NAKED ATTRACTION	104
DENT	106
CLUMSY	108
LITTLE BAT	110
ESTHER PEACHES	111
MOJO	113
HEATING	115
KEEP MUM	117
UNWANTED GIFT	119

SERVICE	121
WHEELBARROW RACE	122
CLOSE ENCOUNTER	124
INDICATORS	126
IT'S GONE	128
HAPPY	130
BUMBLE BEE	132
WHITE NOISE	133
POOR JACK	134
GIFT.	135
I'M HUNGRY	136
PET SHOP	138
THE LITTLE FART THAT WASN'T.	140
POUND SHOP PRINCESS	141
MISS HOME BARGAINS 2022.	143
WHEN I AM GONE	144
OTHER BOOKS BY THE AUTHOR	146
ABOUT THE AUTHOR	148

DRAWING A BLANK – A WORD FROM THE PUBLISHER

This collection contains eighty-eight wonderful new and original poems by poet Laura J. Booker.

Laura has been very prolific with her poetry in such a short writing career.

This collection still has a lot of bite, and with lashings of humour, sometimes dark, sometimes laugh out loud funny, but we know deep down all her many fans will love it.

The title "Drawing A Blank" comes from Laura and I searching for a witty title and even with our great minds it looked like we were "Drawing a Blank." Which I think sums up this book rather well.

It's not blank verse but it's all about the words, the poetry the writing.

There are no thrills, nor bells, or whistles, just the words and poking fun at life as we know it.

SICKY

I am laid here on my sick bed
Feeling pretty ill, I fear
Wondering what you have to do
To get a cup of tea round here?
I've been in here all day
Getting increasingly frustrated
My shrivelled little kidneys
Are feeling pretty dehydrated
I did get up this morning
An emergency food run to the shop
But I got sweaty and peculiar
And felt like I would drop
So I retreated to my boudoir
Where I hoped to receive proper care
But I've been here for a while
With just the cats who sit and stare
They're fed up of waiting for food woman
To go and fill their dish
I can feel the looks they're giving
Telepathically shouting 'fish'!
It seems they are out of luck
If they are expecting a nice dinner
For as long as I'm not up and about
We'll all be getting thinner
When others are ill I brough hot soup
And massages and rubs
But when it's me
There's nowt you see
Except a cat turd in the tub
A little dirty protest
About the lack of food for them
I'd join them but I'd only have

To clean it up missen
So send me help
Come rub my back
And hold my hair back out the loo
I promise if the tables are turned
I'll do the same for you

FLEA IN MY TIGHTS

You'll think me a bit dirty
But all pet owners will confirm
From time to time we get unwanted visitors
Like fleas and worms
I'm very glad to say
The worms have never invaded me
But I'm afraid to say my tights
Seem to be harbouring a flea
It started on my foot
I thought just a little itch
Then I felt it a bit higher
My senses began to twitch
I looked down and there it was
I could see it near my knee
But it was safely on the inside
The bitey little flea
I tried to get it through the nylon
But he could jump pretty high
In seconds I'd lost track
Until I felt it on my thigh
By now my skirts up round my middle
My knickers out for all to see
But I didn't care I needed to find
This pest inhabiting me
I whipped off my tights to get him off
My body in great haste
But by now he'd left a little trail of bites
Around my waist
I was free but oh so itchy
And we all know not to scratch
But at least I'd stopped him there
Before he settled on my snatch!

DRIVING

There's lots of types of drivers
The old dears and white van man
But do you ever stop to wonder
Which one of them I am
Well, you not me I know of course
That I'm a bloody star
You'd know that if you ever got
Stuck behind my car
But what do others think
Of how you navigate the streets
Do you find angry voices follow you?
Do you hear lots of mystery beeps?
I know everyone thinks they are brilliant
But it's very clear to see
That simple statistics show
Not everyone's as good as me
You'll never catch me speeding
My car is way too fast for that
Well, that's not true, not really
As I don't drive like a twat
I'm one of those strange ones
That examiners like the best
I observe all of the rules
Like they want you to on your driving test
In fact, I was so good at it
They all wanted to see
They asked me back seven times
To see the wonder that is me
It was starting to get awkward
I wasn't finding it that funny
If they didn't pass me soon
I was going to run out of money

So, I gave it one last shot
Cos I really wanted to drive
The roads were wet and icy
But we made it out alive
I think I broke their will
I got a 10 out of 10
And they all waved as I drove away
Cos they'd not get me back again

E BAY

I found I was about to win
But I did not know what
It seems I had been on E Bay
Making bids I had forgot
I must have had a tipple
And seen things that caught my eye
But now I am quite sober
I don't think I want to buy
Damn those bloody auctions
It seems I was committed
To buy the flaming stuff
Regardless of whether it fitted
Some rather fabulous high heels
Just two sizes too big
And a black PVC cat suit
With a free waist length blond wig
I don't know what I had in mind
When browsing for these items
Is there a side to me I'm not aware of?
Should I be concerned or frightened?
Clearly drunk me has no shame
And is drawn to S&M
As I've also won some bed restraints
To go along with them
I had better warn the post man
So he doesn't think I'm branching out
Into something more than poetry
It's best there isn't any doubt
I'm going to delete the app
So I don't buy anything more
And I'm going to give up drinking
As drunk me is possibly a whore

TERRIBLE TEMPTRESS

Beware I'm a terrible temptress
That lures unsuspecting men
Into something, I'm not sure what
As I'm fast asleep by ten
But my photos to some seem to suggest
I'm a tart and leading fellas on
But I don't know how I'm doing that
As I've nothing sexy on
My face isn't owt special
And I've nothing on display
I make sure my devil's dumplings
Are safely tucked away
I don't talk about sex and naughty stuff
I write poetry of sorts
And occasionally on a weekend
Get a bit angry about sports
I'm a terrible wife it must be hell
Being wed to me
With all the fellas I'm collecting
I get through five before my tea
I chew them up and spit them out
With no regard for how they feel
Because that's what us temptresses do
Ah, if only any of this were real
Other ladies post their photos
With boobs out or flashing thighs
But a photo of just my head
Is much more dangerous when collecting guys
I've angry wives in my inbox
They seem really pissed
But the only crime I'm guilty of
Is daring to exist

The very cheek of it, naughty me
Surely a harlot such as I
Should wear a sack and live in a cave
And wave you innocent ones goodbye
I must say it's quite perplexing
I'd love to know what I have done
To sit here getting grief
When I haven't even had the fun
Anyway, I'm going back to my temptressing
Yes, I know it's not a word
I'm really blocking the loony wife
Cos that's one insecure and crazy bird

BORED

I'm so blooming bored
I had to check I was still alive
I stuck a pin in my leg
Cos I thought I might have died
There's nothing left to do
On my to do list
I'll just get myself in trouble
Or end up getting pissed
I don't feel like watching telly
I want to do something fun
But I can't think of anything
Except taking pictures of my bum
Maybe I should go dig out
My kids old chemistry kit
I'll mix some bits together
That should spice things up a bit
I've been and had a look
But it's all a mystery to me
And it didn't have instructions
For making home-made ecstasy
I suppose that I could have a stab
At a DIY piercing or tattoo
But my artworks not that good
Could I test it out on you?
I'm feeling quite mischievous
And need a way to pass the time
Unfortunately no one wants to be
My partner in crime
So I'll just sit and pick this skin
On my finger til it bleeds
That's as exciting as it gets
With nothing to fill my boredom needs

I suppose I could do a crossword
And hope this boredom will soon pass
But if it doesn't standby on twitter
For I'll be posting pictures of my ass

VEGAN SWEETS

Why have vegans spoiled our sweeties?
All the flavour is gone
They used to taste all nice
Until the vegans came along
I don't mind a bit of cow in mine
I'll risk mad cow disease
Cos they've gone and taken the flavour out
Can someone put it back? Pretty please?
If you want to be vegan
I applaud you, sincerely well done
But by taking something meaty out
You've spoiled our sweetie fun
If you want to eat all beans and stuff
Go for it, be my guest
But don't go messing with my Haribo
Or drumsticks, they'll be next!
I don't care much what I'm eating
I know the fats and e numbers are rife
But I have kind of got used to them
I've been eating shit all of my life
And don't think I haven't noticed
You're messing with other stuff too
Slipping almond milk in coffee
Even though for some of us, it goes straight through
Just because its vegan doesn't mean
That's it's all good for you
Next time I go to Costa
I don't want an instant poo
So, approach this vegan stuff with caution
This plant based trend is built on lies
Leave my jelly snakes alone
But I will try those vegan fries

WIN THE LOTTO

I'm going to win the lotto
And have a massive spending spree
Not on shoes or liposuction
I'll buy a gin distillery
It's a saving in the long run
And might make me a few bob
But I'll need someone to run it
As I'll be too drunk to do the job
I won't be giving out freebies
Not the centre of good will
It will be time to seek revenge
On those that bear me any ill will
Yes, old karma is a bitch
And so, I will be too
Time for some to feel my wrath
For all the bad stuff that they do
Most people go for holidays
And a big flash four by four
But that's just so predictable
I'm sure I could do more
I'll buy myself an island
And build myself a lair
You know, like in a bond film
So no one could find me there
Of course, I will need a chef
To make my dinner times all swish
Because my squeaky chicken
Is not a popular dish
And naturally I will need a cleaner
That I could follow around
To make sure they did it properly
And show them all the dust I found

I suppose I'll get a man in
To do stuff around the place
I'm not sure what but he would need
A nice bum and pretty face
Perhaps a nice tall Canadian sort
Might fit the person specification
I'll do the interviews now
So I'm ready for the situation
So, when I win the Lotto
You won't see me again
I'll be hiding on my island
With my hordes of servant men

POSTIE PETE

Postman Pete had an unusual gift
He had extremely strong pheromones
Which made him most attractive to dogs
They wanted to give him a bone
Most posties are usually scared of being bitten
Or chased down the garden path
All the pooches wanted a piece of our Pete
Unfortunately, it was his ass
They would pick up his scent at 200 yards
The excitement got them barking and jumping
And when he came through the gate, they just couldn't wait
To give his bare legs a good humping
He tried to distract them with lotions and sprays
To throw the woofers off his trail
But nothing would hide it, they wanted to ride it
His efforts were to no avail
A particular address on his route
Housed a St. Bernard call Mr McFee
It saw him arrive, and in his arms it did dive
And then went to town on his knee
Now St. Bernard's are not very little
It pushed him onto his back
But it had him pinned in, til it had finished with him
And shot it's load onto his sack
Poor postie had had enough of this
He sought him a new occupation
He got a new job, working for a plumber called Bob
Which involved less animal copulation

PARTY FOX VERSUS THE FERAL CATS

There is gang warfare been going on round here
Not with guns or baseball bats
But a furry sort of war
Between Party Fox and feral cats
The fox started the trouble
Nicking pizza remnants out of my bins
And washing it all down
With a couple of Stella tins
It got him a bit lairy
Rolling around drunk on the grass
But it didn't go down well with the feral cats
Who wanted to kick his ass
You see the cats they were more sneaky
Just pinched the odd bone out of the bins
They didn't leave much mess
Didn't leave the garden strewn with things
But the party fox went and spoiled it
As we'd had to clean up his litter
We put bricks on top of the bins
And now the cats were feeling bitter
There was a stand-off in the garden
Fighting for the wheelie bin
Party Fox thought he could take them
But they had brought the cavalry in
All the manky cats from all around
Lined up along the wall
Their claws glinting in the moonlight
Party Fox couldn't fight them all
He made a little foxy scream
A shout out to his mates

But they were busy down the kebab shop
When they arrived, it was too late
Party Fox had met a sticky end
A warning to other naughty foxes
They put him out for recycling
Buried under those pizza boxes
But at least he left this world
Next to the thing he loved the most
And now my wheelie bin is haunted
By a little party ghost

BLOW UP DOLL

I was walking down the street
When a strange thing I did see
In the window of a shop
A shocked face looking back at me
The lips were red and full
Her eyes big and round
She had a very ample bosom
I couldn't believe what I had found
A blow up doll in the charity shop
She'd been used and then got rid
Just the one careful owner
A bargain at five quid
As if this wasn't sad enough
By her side in a crumpled heap
Lay her little companion
A latex blow up sheep
My heart went out to the both of them
Their owner's desires had been sated
And now they were rejected
And just a little bit deflated
What must they both have seen and done?
What went on behind closed doors
And what was dolly doing
While the sheep was on all fours?
Just to make matters worse
And what I really found most shocking
Was the doll had got an apron on
But the sheep, high heels and stockings
I nipped inside to buy a dress for her
And a nice big pair of knickers
But when I tried to give her some dignity
Who was buying the sheep? The local vicar!

He was trying to convince us
It was for the nativity
But I saw that look in his eye
He wasn't kidding me
So, I rescued the blow up doll
So no one could do her ill
You must be bloody crackers
Said the woman on the till
But I'm not as daft as I look
Although some might think I'm crazy
I stick her in bed with my nightie on
When I'm feeling a bit lazy
Then I can get a good night's sleep
And not be rudely awoken
But I keep a puncture repair kit on standby
As one of her valves is broken

OFFER

I had a dodgy offer
Off a funny fella
To go and stay at his house
But I suspected in his cellar
I've never even met the bloke
Not even had a chat
It set alarm bells ringing
As he didn't see anything weird in that
I said, but I am married
My husband won't agree
He said, tell him it's a work thing
Go on, come and stay with me
When I told him it was strange
He might want to do me ill
He got quite offended
As he put down his shovel
But I've already got the duct tape
And the lotion for your skin
Ignore the bin bags in the van
Just shut up and jump right in
I really do not want to
I told him this again
I don't want to be your pet
Or live in your weird sex den
So I left it there and then
No more offers if you will
Go away and find something else to do
Rather than planning your next kill

I'VE KILLED MY CACTUS

I think I've killed my cactus
Given up on keeping it alive
I just don't think I have the skills
For helping things to thrive
I tried growing fruit in the summertime
It didn't go that well
I managed one and a half tomatoes
That gave off a funny smell
Some people have green fingers
And produce a bountiful crop
I just have to look at a plant
And its leaves will drop
My cactuses or cacti
Look like a bunch of shrivelled willies
Or perhaps that should be peni?
Maybe not, that just sounds silly
I may have under watered them
They need assistance something drastic
I think the problem started
When I forgot that they weren't plastic
Maybe I could revive them
With a can of coke
But I'm not holding my breath
I really think that they are broke
Their needles have gone bendy
I think they are really sick
And there's not much point keeping them
If I can't get a decent prick
A plastic one will do the trick
A good wipe down is all it needs
And I'll get a plastic cactus too
That requires zero feeds

STUCK

Pervy people are costing the NHS
Three hundred and fifty grand a year
That's an awful lot of money
For pulling stuff out of their rear
I know it may be tempting
And even seem like fun
To insert random objects
Up yours, or someone else's bum
But the problem is your sphincter
Is really rather strong
You might have hold of things for a second or two
And their suddenly they're gone
Then it's time to visit A & E
And attempt to explain
How amazingly you fell and landed on
A pool cue...again!
You'll be well known with the nurses
A repeat offender
For all those funny accidents
And each one, a rear ender
Do you want to be that person?
Do you want to be famous?
For the amount of things
They've had to extract from your anus?
They have all got better things to do
Than sort out your fun and games
So, if you shove something in
Make sure you can get it out again
By all means do whatever you want
If it gets you feeling randy
But if it goes wrong, I hope you've got rubber gloves
And plenty of Vaseline handy

GREEDY CAT

Greedy little cat
Get your head out of my food
I haven't eaten yet
You are being rather rude
You have eaten several times today
Whilst I haven't had a lot
So stop licking what I made
And get your head out of the pot
I know you think you are starving
And I'm the food serving lady
But I prefer my dinner
While it has still got the gravy
I'd also find it better
If it wasn't covered in cat spit
So get down off the table
You greedy little shit
I'm aware of your presence
You're not invisible to me
I noticed you the fifteen times
You bounced on and off my knee
I noticed you in the kitchen
When round my legs you entwined
Or the other four times I fed you
When I was cooking mine
I even gave you all the scraps
And all the chicken skin
And yet you need to tell me
How you're awfully thin
I assure you, you're not wasting away
So I'll ignore your call
You can wait a bit to eat
You're like a bloody rugby ball

So greedy little cat
Please don't miaow fuss and beg
Get off my chuffing dinner
And give back that chicken leg

MISTRESS K

I'm Mistress Kate Da Demon
A dominatrix, a findom
At least that's what the account said
The one I chanced upon
They've gone and nicked my photo
Telling folk to give me all your money
All BDSM and bondage
Which does seem kind of funny
I never knew I was that kind of girl
I must have missed a trick
So I'm jumping on the bandwagon
As I need some money quick
I'm getting into latex
All rubber hose and heels
And I'll exploit you like you all deserve
Because you got them feels
Go on worship the ground I walk on
Call me a goddess, that's the way
And for the honour of doing so
Get out your cash and pay
You see I'm getting into this
The power is quite appealing
I'm not sure if I should carry on
As a dark side it's revealing
I do wonder though if I was a success
Did anyone actually pay?
Do I have other personas out there?
But maybe not quite that risqué?
Just how many of me are there?
And what are we all into?
Are they all naughty like mistress Kate?
Or are there submissive ones there too?

How many servants do I have?
Is this thing all the rage?
How many fellas think I own
The key to their cock cage?
When really, it's a 6-foot bloke
Sat holding the key
Deceiving them all from afar
With stolen pics of me
It's really quite upsetting
I don't like being exploited in this way
I'm setting up a new account
Mistress K Findom UK

BILLY

The story of Billy an unfortunate lad
Who had an occasional oversized nad
Seems Billy had a strange affliction
Unusually fuelled by his addiction
You see Billy couldn't leave his nuts alone
Not those ones! Before I hear you moan
No, a nut allergy our Billy had
But it only affected his right nad
The left one never changed, nor did his knob
Despite the nuts he shoved down his gob
But the right one, well it was a sight
And stopped him from being upright
It grew to quite epic proportions
Which resulted in painful contortions
It really wasn't a good look
Made worse by the drastic actions he took
To make the swelling go away
He'd have to whip his bits out on display
Then jab it with an EpiPen
Which made him wince a bit and then
His normal sized bullock would be back
That's until he fancied another snack
See our Billy wasn't very bright
Couldn't see his choices weren't quite right
He should have had some crisps or a custard cream
Or at least tried antihistamine
It was all going well until that fateful day
He found he'd accidentally thrown his EpiPen away
Without the drugs to reduce the size
A monster grew between his thighs
His love spud it just grew and grew
And turned a worrying shade of blue

With all the blood in his ball, and not in his head
I'm afraid poor Billy just dropped dead
So, take heed of this tale you found in your phone
And leave your bloody nuts alone

CHIPPY NIGHT

I didn't have owt in for tea
Everyone was moaning 'there's nowt to eat'
So, I went and got us something from the chippy down the street
I'd not been in there before
It was one I hadn't tried
But it looked reyt enough
From what you could see from the outside
A couple of fish and chip specials
And a battered sausage just for me
That should stop the hunger
And get me out of cooking tea
The chips seemed ok and that fish
A bit on the small side
But when I bit into my sausage
A surprise I found inside
Not your average size lump of...fat?
A huge cube of, well...whatever
As the grease ran down my chin and began to gag
Now I'm not feeling right clever
I abandoned the mystery sausage
And stuck with the beans and chips
But as I served them up, upon my plate
Something was poking out a bit
At first, I couldn't tell what it was
But then I realised, it was a little foot
Deep fried but definitely mouse sized
This wasn't good news for my gut
After the obvious events that followed
I went back to the chip shop
And said your special ain't that special
I don't like the garnish you placed on top

The owner wasn't having it
Said I was just being too picky
No one else had complained
He didn't care that I'd been sicky
Didn't even offer me a can of pop
As compensation for my trauma
So, I reported him to environmental health
Don't say I didn't warn ya
But if you like your meaty treats
Maybe this is the place for you?
With lots of added extras
And a sprinkling of mouse poo
There is an element of risk involved
You never know what you will get
Apart from salmonella
I think that one's a safe bet

CULT

I'm going to start a cult
I'm not sure what our thing will be
But it's better than being bothered
By people trying to convert me
I'm going to be the leader
You could be my number two
I'm going to get a special hat
I'll get a smaller one for you
It doesn't seem that hard
I looked it up on Wikihow
We don't have to have an altar
Or start sacrificing cows
I suppose we'll need some rules
Just leave them up to me
And something fabulous to worship
So, I've decided that that's me
The rules will be quite simple
No commandments or original sin
Just honour your wondrous leader
With kebabs, chocolate and gin
You'll have to carry out some rituals
To keep your leader happy
Bring me bearded hockey players for my pleasure
And I'll reward you with rhymes most crappy
So come on, are you going to join me?
You can decide who we let in
You can have a band of hangers on
Just keep your hands off my gin

DUNGEON

Come join me in my dungeon
We'll have lots of fun
I'll tie you up and do
Naughty things to your bum
I won't treat you very nice
Because that's what you deserve
You really should be punished
You dirty little perv
I'll abuse and torment you
Like the filthy creature that you are
You can wear the gimp suit
And I'll put on my latex bra
Lots of people like it
At least that's what I found
Go and ask them, they're still down there
All greased up and tightly bound
They do what their mistress tells them
They'll do anything I say
Lick my boots when they've been bad
I think they like my power play
I know that they enjoy it
You should hear how they squeal
When they're spread-eagled and I gently
Squish their balls with my heel
There's nothing really bad goes on
Just a little spanking and humiliation
Some come and join us for an hour or two
Of bad deeds and penetration
I promise I'll look after you
I take good care of my pets
Just make sure that your safe word
Is one you won't forget

BATTLE OF THE HEATING

There's a battle going on
And I reckon it's nationwide
When it's colder in the house
Than it is outside
There'll be fiddling with the thermostat
Skirmishes with the hive
With the attempt to keep the gas bill down
But trying to stay alive
It doesn't help when some people's
Body temperatures a bit out
Sat around in shorts while the rest of us
Grumble fuss and shout
Get that bloody window shut
You're letting out the heat
I don't care if you are boiling
I can't feel my feet
I'm sat under an electric blanket
With thick socks, gloves and a hat
And I've covered myself in dreamies
Just to get a cuddle off that cat
But then you catch your smart meter
Telling you how much it's all costing
So you turn the heating off again
Until your children need defrosting
Tell them to put another jumper on
And an extra one for bed
But remember to check in on them
To make sure they're not dead
I'm not made of money you know
To pay for all this luxurious heat
Which would you prefer my dear?
To be warm or have stuff to eat?

So forgive me if I'm stingy
And you find me a frustrater
It's just the meter said it's time
That I shut off the radiator

12 DAYS OF CHRISTMAS

On the first day of Christmas
My true love gave to me
A shopping list for goodies
And new lights for the Christmas tree
He'd tangled up the other ones
So we had to cut them off
And we couldn't be arsed to look
For the spare set in the loft
On the second day of Christmas
We had a little spat
Cos he didn't chip in for the shopping
The tight arsed little twat
On the third day of Christmas
I started on the baking
But then we fell out again
Due to the mess that I was making
On the fourth day of Christmas
I got fed up making grub
I told him to stick the baking up his bum
And I pissed off down the pub
On the fifth day of Christmas
There were no five gold rings
Just four carol singers at the door
And none of them could sing
On the sixth day of Christmas
The presents I did wrap
It took me chuffing ages
Cos I'd bought all sorts of crap
On the seventh day of Christmas
I got a bit upset
When the tags fell off the presents
And whose what whose I did forget

On the eighth day of Christmas
I started on the gin
Which I think was a mistake
Judging by the empty bottles in the bin
On the tenth day of Christmas
Yes, I know I missed out nine
That because when the gin ran out
I kept going on the wine
On the eleventh day of Christmas
I put the sprouts on to boil
But I forgot to turn them off
But I don't think that they spoiled
So on the twelfth day of Christmas
I gave up and stayed in bed
I made cheese on toast for dinner
And threw the presents in the shed
I refused to go downstairs
Until the Christmas was all done
Next time I'm going alone to a hotel
So I can have some fun

BARBARA SCARBOROUGH

This is the tale of a femme fatale
Goes by the name of Barbara Scarborough
Has a thing for Captain Birdseye
So, she hangs out round the harbour
Got her eye on all the fishermen
She's had a fling with one or two
Oh who am I kidding she's had the lot
The captains and their crew
Yes, she's free with her affections
She takes care of all the lads
She's been around the block a few times
But never once caught crabs
She snags them with her fishnets
Peeking round the harbour wall
As she cries out 'come and get it here'
Who could resist her siren call?
Of all the ladies that frequent the harbour bar
Old Barbara is just the best
Never once has she refused a sailor
Access to her treasure chest
No one's ever lonely
Barbs is always there to help
Her company given freely
Although she smells of whelks
She'll never give you grief
Cause a scene or a kerfuffle
She's just there to give you light relief
With her own five finger shuffle
If you see Barbara hanging round the boats
Go on, show her a good time
She'll show you all around the slots
And do owt for a 99

BALLS TO CHRISTMAS

Balls to bloody Christmas
And trimming up the tree
I hope you're not expecting
Any Christmas gifts from me
I hope you get tinselitus
And your fairy lights go out
Because I don't feel very festive
Listening to you shout
You've sucked the joy out of the season
My fairy has gone on strike
And the three wise men in my nativity scene
Said you should get on your bike
I've put laxative in the mince pies
You thought it was edible glitter
You'll have time to think about changing your ways
While you're sat there on the shitter
I've eaten all the chocolates
And although I feel quite sick
At least the sugar made me happy
Unlike you, you mardy prick
I'd like to kick you in the baubles
And it's not just because I'm pissed
There's nothing in Santa's sack for you
Cos you're on his naughty list
I'm going away for Christmas
And maybe new year too
I don't know where to yet
But it will be a treat without you
So, enjoy your crappy Christmas
As you can see, I'm not that chuffed
With you, you yuletide fun sponge
Take your turkey and get stuffed

HANGOVER

Oh, hangover from Hell
Are you trying to kill me?
I need to vomit, burp and pee
Simultaneously
It's too much for me to cope with
I can't do it all at the same time
My brain has gone into shutdown
Overloaded by the wine
I was so hot I took my clothes off
As I walked in the door
But now I'm finding it quite chilly
Laid flat out on the bathroom floor
My poor little head is pounding
My legs have got the shakes
And my stomach wants to empty
With every movement that I make
I can't be sick anymore
I've nothing left to give
I'm never doing tequila shots again
For as long as I live
Now I'm just dry heaving
That stage after the yellow bile
Which for some reason tastes like pear drops
I may be here for quite a while
I've been leaning on the toilet bowl
I'm pretty sure I'm almost dead
And there's a pattern that says Armitage Shanks
Imprinted on my head
I know I should drink water
The headache is caused by dehydration
But I can't get up to get some
Or leave my toilet situation

I suppose at least I'll lose some weight
I might look a little thinner
But only as I've unloaded
My breakfast lunch and dinner
Come give me a hand up off the floor
I need medication to feel like new
Just throw a towel down over there
As I might have missed the loo
Plonk me on the bed a while
Make the room nice and cool
Put a wet flannel on my head
And wipe away the drool
I'm never drinking like this again
I'm too old for this malarkey
Let's pretend this didn't happen
Like an MP's Christmas party

TWAS THE FORTNIGHT BEFORE CHRISTMAS

Twas the fortnight before Christmas
And I'd tidied all the house
I found some weird stuff in the cupboard
And what could be a dead mouse
I've hung the stocking by the fireside
Like in the book with extra care
I hope it stays nice and warm now
As I've none left to wear
The children are nestled all snug in their beds
They'll be nice and comfy there
No visions of sugar plums in their heads
Cos I've let em have a beer
When out on the lawn
There was such a din
I'd locked out my old fella
He couldn't get in
Away to the window
I flew like a flash
To say he can stick his lost key
Right up his ass
When what to my wondering eyes should appear?
He waved a kebab and a six pack of beer
I opened the door
And was turning around
When he tripped on the step
And face planted the ground
He was dressed all in black
From his head to his foot
Cos he'd been out on the rob
All the beer offs were shut

A bundle of toys he had flung on his back
I kicked him right out
And said take them right back
A wink of my eye
And a slap to his head
Soon gave him to know
He'd be kipping in the shed
But I heard him exclaim
As he strode out of sight
Merry sodding Christmas
You mardy shite!

SHIT DAY

I'm sorry if this isn't a jolly one
I may whinge and groan a bit
But it's just a few days before Christmas
And it's all gone a bit shit
I didn't get the dream job
I had set my heart upon
Looks like they wanted something different
And as usual I'm not the one
They my car failed it's MOT
It's cost 600 quid to fix
Looks like it's sausages for Christmas day
And Christmas pudding...half a Twix
I must confess I got a bit upset
I had a little strop
They wouldn't accept monopoly money
At the garage or the shop
If it gets worse, I'll be on the game
Not great for a woman like me
I never thought I'd be turning tricks
To pay for my MOT
To make things worse when I got home
My cats had diarrhoea all over the place
And when I tried to scoop it up
Some poo flicked back in my face
I can safely say I'm giving up
I'll try again next year
My life has turned to shit
And there's still a bit behind my ear
So be nice and treat me gently
To odd kind word or two
Cos life's pretty tough, I've had enough
This year was a pile of poo

SALES

I've been perusing the sales
I like a bargain or two
But there wasn't much to choose from
I didn't know what to do
I wandered down the high street
In all the usual stores
When I came across an item
I'd never seen before
They said it was a toy
But it had been out on display
So, there was ninety percent off
As quite a few had had a play
I thought it was quite a bargain
Cheap at half the price
As personal massager
It said it made you feel nice
It had many different settings
Been tested by a few
The assistant said, if you're gonna buy it
I'll wipe it down for you
Oh, don't worry I replied
It looks nice and clean
Oh no, I really think I should, she said
You don't know where it's been
I laughed and said no really
Its only for your back
But she whispered the fella before me
Had had it in his crack
So, I declined her kind offer
And the hefty discount too
And I got myself a fresh one
Well, what's a girl to do?

You always use your Christmas money
To buy yourself new toys
Cos you have to play with yourself
When there's no other girls and boys

GETTING READY

Getting ready for a big night out
Sorting out my bits
Getting out that bra that
Really pushes up my tits
Plucking tinting and waxing
I look like a sheep that's lost its wool
I don't know why I bother
It's not like I'm going on the pull
But I like to be well presented
Up above and down below
Girl guiding taught us to be prepared
Cos I guess you never know
Be just my luck to bump into Daniel Craig
But in my getting ready rush
I forget to do the maintenance
And scare him off with an unkempt bush
I'm primped and preened immaculate
I've never looked this good before
It's a shame I'll look a state
By the time I'm heading out the door
I've even got my fancy undies on
As it makes me feel empowered
I've never been this well presented
I mean come on, I've even showered
I'm wearing my favourite perfume
I'm covered in Chanel
I swear I'll slap anyone that says to me
What's that funny smell?
So, if you seem me out on the town tonight
Give me a compliment or two
Even if I'm all bedraggled
And lost a heel off my shoe

A lot of effort went into this
It only happens once a year
And I'm sure I'll look alright
Well, after a few beers

POEM

I've been trying to write a poem
But I don't know what to write about
I'm trying to think of something smutty
But I just can't knock one out
Someone suggested a Cardiff prozzie
But it just doesn't feel right
I mean how can I get knob
Into a lady of the night?
Another said, a poo adventure?
A doodoo related skit
But I can't find owt funny in it
All my jokes were shit
I thought maybe a little Christmas tale
About Santa and his sack
But it's all empty and saggy just yet
Too early to take it on his back
So, I've given up trying to write owt
I'm going to cook my tea
See if the breast and dumplings
Will inspire me
Or perhaps a nice warm sausage
Shoved between my baps
Or something big and meaty
For my moist lips to wrap
Maybe after I've eaten
I'll start to feel me
And feel the urge to slip one in again
But for now, my heads empty
And I don't like that feeling
I like things in my head
It's just a big hole that needs filling up
So, I'm off now, bye, nuff said

BOXING DAY

Its boxing day, I'm a little full
Not sure what I ate yesterday
But it appears a whole box of chocolates
Seems to have gone away
I had the best intentions
To get out and go for a run
But its pissing it down outside
Indoors seems like much more fun
I've got on my fluffy pyjamas
And there's pastries to be eaten
I don't think that I'll be going soon
It's still the Christmas season
The stresses have all gone away
Now we're just playing with games
To spoil it all with exercise
Well, it seems a shame
I'm sure James Bond is one somewhere
He can do the action bit for me
I'm going to see how many types of meat
I can eat for my tea
I'm all cheesed out; I can take no more
My stomach is in distress
But I must eat anything that's perishable
Best finish that trifle while it's fresh
I'll start the diet tomorrow
Or maybe in the new year
Cos I need a good rest anyway
And I need another beer
Boxing day is meant for food and sports
And watching rubbish telly
And burping and drinking Andrews
While someone rubs your belly

So, are you coming round to help me?
The monopoly is safely put away
And I'll save the naked twister
For at least another day

CHRISTMAS EVE

It's Christmas Eve, it's getting late
It is nearly time for bed
It's time to have a lot of rum
And lay down your weary head
Don't forget to leave a carrot
And a mince pie and a drink
Cos he'll be hungry when he gets here
I heard he likes gin, nudge nudge wink wink
But don't get yourself too plastered
Remember there are quiet jobs to be done
Don't go crashing about on the landing
Or Christmas morning won't be fun
Daddy, why does Santa swear so much?
Your children will ask of you
And what's a bastard nerf gun?
Did he leave one for you too?
I'm sure you'll all be going to midnight mass
Trying to look sincere
And pretending that you're a regular
Though you only go once a year
Be ready to rise at 4am
And be jolly and full of beans
Don't let the kids find you sprawled on the sofa
Dressed in a Santa hat and just your jeans
When the fun starts, remember to be polite
The visitors won't stay forever
And play nice cos throwing the monopoly board
In the air is not big or clever
Help out with the cooking and wash the pots
Don't let that fairy liquid be out of reach
No sneaking off down the pub
In the middle of the queen's speech

So merry Christmas one and all
I'll raise a glass to everyone
Cherish every single minute
Because before you know it, it'll be gone
I wish you all the happiness
And all your heart's desire
Warm hugs and kisses near the mistletoe
And cuddles by the fire
And for anyone alone
On this Christmas day
I wish you peace and joy
And we your friends, aren't far away
But don't think I'm getting soppy
Or trying to get on the nice list
I've been drinking Baileys since my breakfast
I may be a little Brahms and Liszt

LITTLE BOY

He's the little boy that Santa Claus forgot
And I know they said he didn't want a lot
He sent a note to Santa for an X-box and a gun
It broke his little heart when Santa said, tough luck son
Cos on the street you bullied all those other boys
You nicked their money and trampled on their toys
I'm not sorry for you laddie, you're a proper little baddie
The little boy that Santa Claus forgot
He went to his dad and said, sort this Santa out
He doesn't know who we are
He's gone and brought me nowt
His dad who was a dealer said, I'll go and fix it son
You fetch the baseball bat, and I'll go and get my gun
But when they knocked on Santa's door they were surprised
They were met by a dozen burly guys
You see Santa's not a sucker, he's a well hard mother f****r
Ready for the little boy that Santa Clause forgot
So, they ran away with their heads hung in shame
With those big fellas chasing them down the lane
They put down their weapons
And thought about how they'd been done
And the dad said to his lad, ah forget about it son
I'll buy the X box myself and a gun too
Cos nobody tells us what to do
Don't feel sorry little laddie
You've got a drug dealer gangster daddy
You'll be the little boy that got an awful lot
But they got a shock when they got back home
For Santa had been busy on the phone
His daddy was disgusted
To find out that he'd been busted
Turns out that Santa remembered an awful lot

So, for anyone wondering what to do
Make sure you're nice not nasty
And your thoughts are true
Don't be mardy or throw a paddy
Like that young lad and his daddy
Or Santa will leave your tangerines to rot

STICKY END

Whilst flicking through the paper
I glanced at the obituary
And found something quite intriguing
Now a new hobby for me
We just assume people 'go' in the usual ways
A long illness or old age
Turns out there's some juicy stories
Hidden in that page
Poor George he met a sticky end
He takes the top ranking
He died from dehydration
Brought on by excessive wanking
But he's not the only sex mishap
Take poor Mary and her bondage tricks
She got hiccups and swallowed the ball from her gag
It got stuck between her lips
Her fella Naughty Nigel
Thought she was trying asphyxiation
He didn't help till it was way too late
Had fun explaining that one down the station
Yes, hidden in the papers
There's all sorts of sordid tales
The things people get up to
It's a wonder they're not in jail
And that's just the ones that make it
And give the ambulance crew a shock
Unlike poor Dave who attached
A car battery to his cock
Someone told him it would be such a buzz
He felt very naughty indeed
He'd never thought that that crocodile clip
Would cause such a bleed

He never got to feel the buzz
He didn't get turned on
Passed out as he chopped his bell end off
And now poor Dave is gone
So, take heed from all these tales of woe
Don't let this happen to you, or me
Keep away from naughty antics
Or we'll be one of 'those' obituaries

HOBBIES

My other half is a mardy bugger
A real grumpy git
So, I've arranged him some new hobbies
To get him out the house a bit
A bit of paragliding
ought to be a treat
It should hopefully clear his head a bit
And get him out from under my feet
I know it's a bit dangerous
But some risks are worth taking
I even bumped the insurance up
In case some mistakes he be making
Next up is some potholing
Deep, deep underground
He can grumble all he wants down there
I won't hear a sound
And then I've booked skydiving
I reckon that will be a hoot
If he's good, I'll push the boat out
And throw in a parachute
So, I've done land and air
I'd better add some deep-sea diving
I've covered all the bases
I can't see him surviving
I think he'll get the message
To stop with the whinging and the dramas
When he finds his swim with the dolphins
Is really swimming with piranhas

A NEW HOBBY

I sought out a new hobby
To give me something new to do
I wanted to set free my creative side
But didn't have a clue
I went down the community centre
There was a class that caught my eye
Life drawing for beginners
I thought I'd give that one a try
I sharpened up my pencils
And got a few sheets of A3
Cos I needed something to hide behind
In case I felt a bit giggly
I know I really shouldn't
And its nervousness that's all
But I'm not used to naked Pauline
Getting it all out in the church hall
She was certainly enthusiastic
Pauline had no inhibitions
I was soon engrossed in capturing her
In all her strange positions
I was starting to impress myself
But that was up until when
Someone else joined naked Pauline
It was...naked Ken
What's wrong with that? Well, nothing
Not for the others in the class
But for me it wasn't the first time
I'd seen naked Ken's bare ass
You see Ken and I had been intimate
Not long after I'd left school
I'd lent him my big rubber
And he gave me his slide rule

It would appear he'd grown a bit
Which I found somewhat distracting
I drifted off and thought of other scenes
That we could be enacting
So, I've hung up my pencils
I'm back to just using my pen
But not just yet I've got a date
With not so naked Ken

RUN

While out jogging on New Year's Day
I found a few worrying items that had been thrown away
It became apparent for all to see
Someone had had a better New Year's Eve than me
The first item I came upon
Was a dressing gown belt on the floor flung
Someone had clearly cast their clothes aside
And skipped naked down the road with pride
How did I know this was a nudie dance?
Because they had also discarded their underpants
Not the cleanest pair I must confess
The state of them caused me much distress
I wondered how far they'd got down the road
Because last night was pretty cold
But it seems they didn't get that far
Because a few feet away I found a soggy bra
The clothes free pair must have had some fun
Cos next I found a used condom
It wasn't pleasant finding an old Johnny in the street
I nearly slipped on it beneath my feet
It wasn't the enjoyable run I had in mind
So, I moved quickly to leave their stuff behind
When the final item in my haul
I found placed carefully on a wall
What wondrous item for my treasure chest?
But a positive lateral flow test
In suppose given the night they must have had
Just catching covid might not be that bad
So next time I'm out for exercise
I think I just might close my eyes

WHEN YOU'RE OLD

When you're old you get to be naughty and get away with it
And it's okay to not bother getting dressed and smell a bit like shit
If you want to keep your nightie on when going down the shops
That's ok you can leave your slippers on too and just wear a woolly coat on top
If your hair's gone mad just cover it up with any old bobble hat
Everyone will just say aww bless how cute
They won't tell you, you look a twat
You can have your programmes on as loud as you want and ignore everything except the telly
Cos you're pretending you just can't hear them, that is until they offer you a glass of sherry
You'll be off your head on drugs, so many you'll forget what they're all for
You don't have to go out to score or anything, they deliver them to your door
The kids won't suspect a thing, they think you know nothing cos your old and lame
They'll never guess you have blown their inheritance on some online poker game
Its ok to get a bit grumpy, people just smile and shake their head
And you take pleasure from reading the obituaries and seeing whose dropped dead
Aha you think the bastards, they always thought they were better than me
Who's having the last laugh now when they're a goner by seventy-three

Don't judge me though by these things I say I'll do in thirty years
Just bring me a sherry and turn the telly up, that's if I'm still here

MONEY

I need to make some money
I have a lot of debt
I know some folk turn to only fans
But I haven't sunk that far yet
And anyhow I don't have the equipment
To support that kind of stuff
People would want a refund
If they saw me in the buff
I tried to think of stuff that I can sell
With no real talent, looks or wit
My only hope is these here poems
And even they are shit
I was going to sell a kidney
Turns out only one of them is good
So, I think I'd best hang onto it
Does anyone buy blood?
Years ago, folks as skint as I am
Would sell their teeth or hair
But that market, like me has all dried up
No one wants to buy my wares
So, you seem my options are quite limited
No organ harvesting or naughty vids
I don't fancy prostitution
So, I'll just have to sell my kids

RAGE

We're not supposed to get grumpy
Everyone tells us to just smile
But I'm sorry but somebody
Just really gets me riled
I'm not a nasty person
I think of others before me
But it doesn't half get on my tits
Being asked what's for tea?
Did you pick my beers up?
What have we got to eat?
Have my trousers been washed?
Rub my shoulders and my feet
It's no wonder that I fantasise
About doing evil deeds
And while I do more, and they do less
The more resentment breeds
But I'm not here to have a moan
That's not the purpose of this rhyme
I just want to get on record
If I crack the faults not mine
I'll be sure it looks like an accident
Some unexpected tragedy
And even if that doesn't wash
I'll claim diminished responsibility
But you had better be my alibi
You know just to back me up
We'd better get a good old story
For that ground glass in his cup
Who would have thought that anvil
I was balancing on the door
Would have had a little wobble
And knocked him through the floor

Or the brakes suddenly stop working
The toaster slips into the bath
Or someone remove the manhole cover
You know just to have a laugh
All believable scenarios
That could happen to anyone
But if anyone should ask
We were out the whole day long

WORK

Please tell me why I work
I think I've got it wrong
I get very little sleep
And I'm busy far too long
There are people never had a job
Got bigger houses than me
And flashy motors too
What did I do wrong? I can't see
I earn too much to get benefits
But not enough for the good things
I'm scrimping and saving every month
While the others live like kings
I get up about five thirty
To squeeze the exercise in
Then its work, shop, cook, clean, run around
With barely time for gin
My nails they are in tatters
No time for appointments for my hair
While lady muck down the road
Drives her BMW without a care
The numbers just aren't adding up
I daren't look at the tax I pay
To fund Madame Tracksuit's need
To sit on her fat arse all day
I wouldn't say I'm bitter
I don't make big demands
But how can the couple that have never worked
Take their kids to Disneyland?
I've never had one day's benefit
Never signed on in my life
But these workshy gits are everywhere
And causing me great strife

It's just all so unfair
Where's my reward for working hard
When I drop dead at work
I'm sure they won't even send a card
Come on give me a year off taxes
Give this girl a hand
And let me take my kid somewhere nice
Let's all go to Disneyland

GOD OF POO

While sitting on the toilet
Feeling rather glum
I wondered why nothing seems to be
Coming out my bum
I thought I needed fibre
To relieve the situation
Maybe I haven't moved enough
Or perhaps its dehydration
As I clenched and strained
I turned to the heavens to ask why
Could I get any assistance
From the god of jobbies in the sky?
So, sitting there just waiting
All bored, bunged up and alone
I tried to pass the time
By playing on my phone
Don't ask what I was googling
When sitting on the loo
But I discovered Zigu
The Chinese God of Poo
It seems the bog is occupied
By three sisters all holy
And we are all descended
From a celestial toilet bowly
I know what you are thinking
You couldn't make up this shit
But I was in there for some time
So, I researched it quite a bit
The Māori have poo rituals too
They take a bite of the latrine
It transfers powers or summat like that
Sounds like a weird fetish scene

I go so into reading poo tales
I lost the urge to go
So, I had to summon all my strength
To try to, well, you know
I should have brought an offering
To appease the Gods of Plop
I should have also brought a toilet roll
When I went for this big shop
But the sisters of the cistern
Were not playing nice that day
So, I left to get some senna pods
And try again another day

MUCKY BILL THE BUTCHER

Have you met mucky Bill the butcher?
Makes burgers out of rats
Sets traps around the bins to catch them
Them and dogs and cats
His sausages are famous
I don't know what they're made of but it's not meat
My guess is bone and gristle, they're all grey and smell like feet
Not many normal folk visit his shop, they see his meat and turn away
But I guarantee you've eaten it, as he supplies the local takeaways
His hygiene rating isn't that good, he's just lost the one star
Apparently, venison isn't fit for use when it's been scraped off the bottom of the car
He gets his meat from everywhere, the road, the abattoir
And the pigeons off the phone line that keep pooping on his car
I know it sounds quite nasty but honestly, it's not that bad
You seemed to enjoy it the other night when you tucked into that kebab

ANAL

I had a little cock up
Tweeted about an email finger slip
Where I made an unfortunate type
Ten thousand likes it hit!
Seems that the word anal
Had got everyone's attention
So much that I had to perform
A mute tweet intervention
I wondered how a simple tweet
Could plunge the depths of twitter
Why the bizarre fascination
With taking it up the shi.... bum
So now I'm on a mission
It's a little bit absurd
To discover what else does it
What are the trigger words?
I'm going for the obvious ones
Ménage a trios, feet and spank
And of course, Justin Bieber
You can take that to the bank
See you weren't expecting the last one
I'm not a fan but that one's a banker
And you can swap his name for any other
Teen girl crush pop wanker
I'm going to work out the formula
So every tweet's a hit
It's easier than writing stuff
Or showing nudey bits
I'll become a social media hit
I'll be on that trending page
With my fetish laden tweets
Just 'cum' and see it's all the rage

So wish me luck as I set out
On my fearless journey brave and bold
I'm just off to write a sonnet
About whips and cuffs and a cuckold

CREATURE

Fifteen years ago today
I felt a little twinge
And then the urge to push
A little creature out my minge
Labour was not fun
It went on for quite a bit
Then they picked the creature up
And attached it to my tit
A funny little thing it was
It's head shaped like a cone
They gave it a wipe down
And told me to take it home
I didn't know what to do with it
It just ate and slept and pooed
But I thought I'd best not take it back
As that might seem quite rude
So, I kept it safe and warm
And tried to keep it well
And I loved that little creature
In spite of the smell
It started to get bigger
And roam about the place
It started eating all my treats
And rubbing chocolate on its face
It was kind of endearing
This grubby little mess
And who could resist it's cuddles
Despite the stains on my dress
But now the creature is all grown up
Fifteen years old today
And even though it doesn't cuddle much
I still feed it every day

It may have sleeping sickness
As it doesn't crawl much out of its pit
But when it does it's pretty nice
And it's lost the smell of shit
So, I think that I shall keep it
Til it grows up and moves away
And sneak those crafty cuddles in
Especially now on its birthday
Cos to me it is and will always be
That little creature on my chest
Who I love much more than life itself
As my creature is the best.

TOILET

I'm not cleaning the toilet
I'm not doing it anymore
Because I don't pee on the seat
And I don't pee on the floor
I don't know what you do in there
To achieve the heights you do
And I'm not just referring to number ones
I'm talking number two
We have shared bodily fluids
Which is fine to a degree
But I draw the line at poo splats
And your artwork made of wee
I know you are a bit that way inclined
Perhaps it was a Jackson Pollock imitation
But I'm not into piss play
So, here's the bleach and an invitation
To clean the bloody mess yourself
You can see just what you've done
It's all yours so clean it up
You'll find it such good fun
Perhaps next time you go
You could move the toilet seat
And not see if you can piss in there
From beyond a couple of feet
If you want target practice
I'll add a ping pong ball
Just to make it more exciting
Maybe you could get some up the wall
So, I'm not cleaning the toilet
Let's see how long you last
Before you realise it's not nice to see
The products of your ass

FLASHER

While walking down the high street
I encountered something silly
A man was stood there showing
What appeared to be his willy
He didn't seem excited
As there wasn't that much there
Or maybe it just shrivelled
With my disapproving glare
He just stood there sort of limp
As he cast a nervous glance
With his little chipolata
Just dangling from his pants
Had I caught an awkward moment?
What was he doing? It was hard to say
Maybe he'd simply forgotten
To do his trousers up that day
I'd assumed flashers would make a point
Of showing you their genitalia
With his little sausage and withered fruit
This flasher seemed like quite the failure
I decided this must simply be
An unfortunate wardrobe malfunction
That also had the effect of
Putting me off my luncheon
I didn't fancy those scotch eggs
Or my bite sized sausage roll
I just walked away and politely said
Put your mole back in the hole

ONLY GRANS

Listen to my tale, it's not a scary un
It features a certain octogenarian
A lady with talents that can't be denied
On account of what she gets 'inside'
To share her talents with
Her legion of fans
Naughty Nelly set up a site
On Only Grans
It attracted those with a special taste
That weren't put off by a wrinkly...face
In fact, her looser skin is what made her famous
Gave her greater stretch on her vag and anus
Strange things she would insert
To her fans delight
She got loads up there
As it wasn't that tight
You might think it might give her a cramp
She even squeezed in a bedside lamp
Of course, those videos you had to buy
To fund her significant lube supply
At her age things were a little dry
As moisture was in short supply
One day she had a misadventure
When she realised, she had lost her dentures
Getting them out really wasn't fun
But not many folk can say, they've bitten their own bum!
Naughty Nelly was blown away
With what she found up there that day
A treasure trove she did uncover
Of things left up there by her lover
A bottle, a rope, she also did find
All accidentally left...behind

Why she'd not noticed them before she couldn't say
But she held an auction on E bay
She made a fortune so with her new income
Retired from Only Grans and sticking stuff up her bum
She still does it sometimes
Just for a select few chaps
Who buy what she produces
From her flaps
A proper 'niche' market you might say
And Naughty Nelly really makes them pay

OUCH

Oh, nasty little wisdom tooth
Although you are so small
You're making me want to take my head
And smash it through a wall
I've taken every drug I can
To alleviate the pain
I'm considering home dentistry
As you are driving me insane
The dentist they can't see me
For another week or two
Even though I rang up crying
Now what am I to do?
I've tried the heat packs, tablets too
I'm considering trepanning
And going downtown to score some stronger drugs
Is what I'm planning
The stabbing, shooting, boring pain
Is making me so ill
Someone rip the bastard out
Because I've really had my fill

ALIEN ABDUCTION

I think aliens abducted me
I don't know where I've been
I woke up during team meeting
All confused like a bad dream
I must have been taken far, far away
In their UFO
And they must have wiped my memory
Cos what they did there, I don't know
One minute I was in there
Doing the agenda setting
Then I woke up with a start
But where I'd been I keep forgetting
They must have taken all of us
As no-one noticed I was gone
And when I went to the loo and noticed too
My pants were on all wrong
I knew I was somewhat sleepy
When I got dressed today
But I'm pretty sure I managed to
Put my knickers on the right way
My undies were on back to front
And there's a mark on my butt cheek
And I know from on the X Files
That's where they drug you to have a peek
The other thing I noticed
Whilst in the middle of disrobing
Was that my bum was really sore
Like I'd just had a good probing
Maybe they had their alien way with me
There's weird gurgling in my tummy
Perhaps I'll birth their big-headed babies
I'm feeling distinctly funny

I'm pretty sure I was abducted
The truth is out there innit?
But I've checked the meeting notes
And it says nothing in the minutes
But I'm ready now in case they
Try to do that shit again
I've got making tin foil hats
As agenda item number ten

MADAME TRACKSUIT

Madame Tracksuit she's a stunner
Her beauty unsurpassed
The only thing bigger than her ego
Is her big, dimpled fat ass
More orange than an Oompah Loompa
With lashings of fake tan
She sits around the house all day
With scroty tracksuit man
They strut round like they own the place
He walks like he's ten men
And she gives the evil eye
To all the regular women
Her massive bun atop her head
Hair an unnatural shade of black
And a skimpy little thong
Stretched to capacity up her crack
With eyebrows like two dead slugs
And lips like suction cups
And a double boob situation
Just to finish off the look
In her mind she's like the girls
On the telly or in magazines
But this one's 'Made in Donny'
But she's still living the dream
She doesn't have a job
She is a kept woman, don't you know?
As scroty tracksuit man sells
Coke to kids and grows some blow
So, watch out for Madame Tracksuit
In her fake designer clothes
Get out of her way as she's all fired up
With what she's had up her nose

And beware scroty tracksuit man
Because he's got a baseball bat
He keeps it by the bed
As he's a little scaredy cat
Not to fend off the gangsters
Although there are plenty of those
It's to keep away Madame Tracksuit
In case she takes off her clothes

CAT EXPLOSION

My little cat exploded
On the floor and up the wall
With what shot out of him
It's a wonder he's still here at all
It wasn't just the once
He came back for an encore
Now my rug isn't as pretty
As it once was before
I thought something wasn't right
While sat watching telly
I got the sense from far away
He had manufactured something smelly
I went to do a reccy
As he wouldn't look me in the eye
I knew it must be bad
But when I saw it my oh my!
Not a single solid to be seen
And not a drop in his litter tray
But there was a puddle by my shoes
And an impressive uphill spray
He had pebble dashed the wall
And left pooey footprints on the rug
He looked so sad and sorry
But I daren't give him a hug
His little belly round and bloated
He was a proper sorry sight
So, I shoved him in my daughter's bedroom
In case he did another in the night
I know you'll think that's mean
But I think I've done my cleaning bit
After all she wanted a cat
So, it can be her puddle of shit

TREVOR

Poor Trevor the snail is not that well
He's retreated back into his shell
And there's a funny smell
I think he may be dead
Usually he's big but now he's small
Just a tiny shadow on the wall
His body is barely there at all
And I can't see his head
Oh Trevor what did we do wrong?
To make your lifetime not that long?
And make you create that awful pong?
Should I bury you by the shed?
But what if you've just begun to hibernate?
And I've already assumed your fate
Or maybe you're trying to escape
By being planted in a flower bed
What if I'm wrong and you're alive?
And in the garden you revive
And take on many. many wives
And your babies are cross bred?
I'll damage the whole food chain
By being a bit previous with your remains
Maybe I should just drop you down the drain
Or squash your little head
Oh Trevor, I don't want to dishonour
Your memory cos you're a goner
I want you to survive I really wanna
But oh Trevor, I think you're dead
Goodbye Trevor I will miss your slime
We loved you for a... short time
I can't find anything else to rhyme
I'm sorry you're brown bread

SKINNY STEVE

I want to tell you about Skinny Steve
A metabolism like you would not believe
He ate all day, imagine that
Yet never gained an ounce of fat
He gorged on cakes and custard creams
And yet he still fit in kid's sized jeans
He tried all sorts to build his size
Protein, Guinness and lots of pies
He tried building muscle down the gym
But that just made him even more thin
Some fella with biceps like the hulk
Offered him some stuff to increase his bulk
But it did nothing to build his mass
And he couldn't find a weight gain class
Skinny Steve was feeling awfully glum
And he sat and cried (on his skinny bum)
He increased his calories to ten thousand a day
Excess it seemed the only way
He ate until he could eat no more
But one day they found him on the floor
You see all that food had made him ill
And now he takes cholesterol pills
His weight gain quest? Well, he's had enough
He knows he will never be big and buff
But it's not all bad as he met Wobbly Winnie
Who prefers her fellas nice and skinny
The perfect pair, the two extremes
But the answer to each other's dreams
He loves her so, though he can't quite embrace her
And she loves him back, her little chubby chaser

VIKINGS

I'm going on a rampage
Just like those Viking hordes
Not because I want to get stuff
It's mostly cos I'm bored
I think that I shall just attack
A little nearby village
And just charge around a bit
I don't intend to pillage
I don't have a Viking longboat
But don't worry as I shall
Sneak up in my rubber dinghy
I'll sail down the canal
I'm pretty sure there is Viking blood in me
As I've always got the horn
But I don't have a helmet
Or even know what they'd have worn
But I have always felt at home
Brandishing an axe or a blade
So, this little Viking is off to find
Somewhere smallish to invade
I've changed my name to blood axe
I'm all fired up and full of beer
You can join me in my dinghy
If you fancy bringing up my rear

BEAUTY NIGHT

I decided on a little treat
A little pamper sesh
I was feeling a bit grotty
Starting to look a mess
I thought enough is enough
I got all my products out
The exfoliators, moisturisers, lotions
Perfumes and grout
I luxuriated in bubbles
Lit a candle played some tunes
A very chilled out situation
Going on in the bathroom
I scraped off all the grotty bits
A felt fresh as a new-born
I went as far as shaving my legs
And sorting out the lady lawn
My hair was teased to perfection
My lashes a sight to behold
A felt a million dollars
Rather than a million years old
But then I went a step too far
I decided on false nails
What followed can only be described
As a completely epic fail
The first hand was fantastic
Long talons full of gems
But the other hand was a different story
I got halfway through and then
The glue shot out quite quickly
I think premature ejaculation
And left my fingers super sticky
Which didn't help the situation

Three fingers stuck together
Which I couldn't separate
I tried soaking in warm water
But I fear it was too late
I tried turps and nail remover
But the glue it was resisting
The only thing my hand was good for
Was giving out a proper fisting
I was overcome with panic
An increasing sense of dread
As I ripped my hand apart
Leaving bits of finger on the bed
I lost all the effects
Of my glamour pamper sesh
With my fingers free of fingerprints
I was in muchos distress
I had to medicate a little
To get over the ordeal
Next time I'll go to the salon
If my fingers ever heal

ROGER THE CHICKEN

Poor Roger the chicken
The unlucky chuck
He found one day
He had lost his cluck
With his little pecker
He searched everywhere
Even up his derriere
Not a sound could he make
Not a single cluck
Roger was sad
Poor little schmuck
His owner he was most perplexed
Why Roger the chicken was feeling vexed
He wondered if there was a sneaky fox
That had scared the cluck from his voice box
Perhaps Roger had an obstruction
Causing the loss of noise production
Was he upset or perhaps distressed?
He didn't know what to suggest
So, to the vet he took our Rog
In case there was something to dislodge
He looked in his eyes and down his throat
But was at a loss, he couldn't see owt
So, he stuck a finger up his bum
Poor Roger was scared as to what might come
His owner had done this before
And what followed left him feeling awfully sore
But the worst didn't happen on this occasion
The vet pulled something out, he felt a sense of elation
It seems his cluck was merely muffled
And although his feathers were slightly ruffled
His cluck was back, it had just been kept at bay

By a used rubber left inside one day
It seems to his owner, he was finger lickin
As he actually did, Roger the chicken
The vet was truly horrified
At what he had just found inside
He took Roger home, this kind stranger
And his cluck came back when safe from danger
But what of his owner, did he go free?
No, he was charged with bestiality

DOG POO

If you have a little doggy
Please explain to me
What is the point of leaving poo bags
Hanging on a tree?
You leave them dangling there
Like decorations on a Christmas tree
But it's not really that festive
Although a little chocolatey
I know it's not the nicest thing
To have to carry round
And I suppose hanging it on high
Is safer than leaving it on the ground
But what do you think will happen
When you suspend it high up there?
Do you think fairies come and get it
To decorate their hair?
You do realise it will hang there
Until the bag is no more
And the doggy doo inside
Falls out and ends up back on the floor
So just do the decent thing
And take it home with you
I haven't got a dog
And I don't need any dog poo
I must say I have had nicer gifts
I like stuff sparkly and pretty
I'm afraid I will have to refuse
Anything soft and shitty
So, take home your little parcels
Of your warm doggy eggs
So, when some of us go running
It doesn't end up on our legs

ALEXA

I wrote a poem called Alexa
To see how much trouble, I could cause
If I threw in random instructions
Part way through...Alexa pause
I know it's a bit naughty
And it might spoil your fun
But I really couldn't help myself
Alexa, please call mum
I could affect your favourites
Alexa play Barry Manilow
Or get you into trouble
Alexa turn the lights down low
But the best idea I had
Was to order stuff for you
Alexa buy a ten inch dildo
And one for Grandma too
And don't forget to get the most
Out of these embarrassing situations
Alexa, please turn on
All delivery notifications
I hope you like my poem
And the Alexa fun it brings
So, as I go, I've just one more ask for her
Alexa where can I buy cock rings?

VALENTINE

To my true valentine who is out there
Wherever you may be
I just know you'll be the sort
To make me egg and chips for tea
I know you'll do it properly
With white bread and lots of butter
I'm just hoping you're the real deal
And not some kind of nutter
I will return the favour
I'll make you loads of fancy grub
And after you have tasted it
We can have some nice food down the pub
I'll give you a nice rub down
I'll even massage your feet
I'll be the perfect partner
Once we eventually meet
You don't need fancy restaurants
Or posh chocs to get in my knickers
Just buy me a can of pop
And a multipack of snickers
I don't want roses either
As pollen makes me sneezy
And forget about the card
Their verses are always cheesy
Just give me unbridled passion
And a heart that's true
And a damn good seeing to
Is what I will offer you
So sweet valentine, my love
I'm sat here ready and waiting
Please be on your way
And not in your bedroom, masturbating

PENI

What is the collective noun for penis?
Is it penises or just peni?
Cos there's an awful lot of pricks about
More than a few but I don't know why
They seem to be just everywhere
All penising about
Spoiling people's days
The dicks are grumpy and like to shout
Why can't they just be nice?
Get on with life and do their job
Instead of picking on us non peni
And acting like a nob
They are spoiling all the good times
By being all loud and silly
And saying stuff that doesn't make sense
Acting like a horse's willy
So, all you penis people
Creating tension and division
Get back inside your pants
Or I'll perform a circumcision

OLD

My daughter and her mate
Put a lovely question to me
Now that you are old
Exactly who do you fancy?
Do you look at fellas in their seventies
And think phwoar they are fit?
How old do they think I am?
I know I'm getting on a bit
But they spoke like old aged pensioners
Are my age the cheeky chuffs
So I said, no I like them in their twenties
While they are still fit and buff
The look of sheer disgust
On their faces was a treat
Then I praised the ones they fancy
They made a hasty retreat
I'd like to think I have managed
To avoid further fun
By enthusiastic perving
Over their favourite actor's bum
It had another advantage
As it put them off their tea
They'll think twice before they ask
Anything else of me
But I'm saving my best moment
For when we next go to the cinema
When their favourite crush appears on screen
I simply will go grrrr!

NORMAN THE SEAGULL

A friend of mine, Mark, lives by the sea
He has a little quandary
A visitor to his cat flap
Wants feeding so he goes tap, tap, tap
Not a kitty as you may have guessed
But one who can leave quite the mess
Norman the seagull an uninvited guest
Known to leave the occasional dirty protest
If nice treats and snacks do not come
He'll decorate your motor with his bum
Now Mark, he is quite a tolerant chap
But not that keen on seagull crap
He is feeling a sense of irritation
At Normans methods of persuasion
Yet doesn't want folk to think he's mean
But he is sick of trying to keep his car clean
In an attempt to repel Norman, the dirty bird
He gave him kippers dipped in lemon curd
That will sort him out he thought with glee
As Norman tucked in enthusiastically
But his smile disappeared as Norman took flight
And covered his car in yellow shite
Mark didn't like his car all plastered
He learned at mind games Norms the master
So now Norm gets fed twice daily no need to pester
And Mark has a nice clean Ford Fiesta

NAKED ATTRACTION

So, I finally bit the bullet
A telly visual distraction
I finally succumbed to
Watching naked attraction
I knew what it was all about
I'd heard about it off my mum
A cheesy dating show
With choices based on their front bum
The heads were hidden from the ladies view
Just a line of todgers on display
And she perused the chaps on offer
And one by one sent them away
They all seemed proud of their tackle
Some were big and some were small
She was surprisingly drawn to the whoppers
All lined up against the wall
She got it down to just two pricks
And it seemed that they both were
By the way that they reacted
When they saw naked her
I really didn't get it
She didn't rate their smiles or their eyes
All of her decision making
Was based on what hung between their thighs
I think she should have been more concerned
About the fact she didn't see
Anything wrong with dating a dude
That gets his junk out on TV
And tell me how can anyone
Tell if they've pulled a cracker
When all you've got to go on
Are a couple of saggy knackers?

I honestly think for real love
If you are trying to befriend them
It's really not the best idea
To show em your pudendum
I know I am the odd one out
A romantic soul at heart
I like to wait at least a day
Until I whip em aht!
Just imaging thirty years from now
With their grandchild upon their knee
What did you think when you first saw Grandma, Pops?
Oh, her flange was such a sight to see!
So, I'm going to stick with Gardeners World
At least I'll get some useful tips
And any growers or indeed showers
Won't involve strangers' dangly bits

DENT

This morning when I awoke
There was an indentation in my head
I didn't know what it was from
I was just glad I wasn't dead
But then I started thinking
What had been happening in the night?
Had someone planned to kill me?
Or perhaps just give me a fright?
It lasted a few hours
So, the pressure was quite great
It's a good idea I woke up then
Or it might have been too late
Were the cats seeking revenge?
For me feeding the wrong sort of food?
Are they the two out of ten cats that don't prefer it?
Did I put them in a mood?
Perhaps I had been sleep walking
And walked into the door
But I still suspected foul play
As I'd never done that stuff before
I analysed the dent
In true CSI style
And while staring in the mirror
Spied something that really made me smile
The dent was quite circular
There was a pattern I could see
What kind of fiendish weapon
Had left its mark on me?
With the aid of a mirror
And a torch to shed some light
I transpired that I hadn't been involved
In some nocturnal fight

The writing was on the wall
Well actually on my head
It said, Gordons, turns out the bottle top
Had been sticking in my head
And no, I'd not been drinking in bed
Well at least not on that day
I'd been flicking it for the cats
And they had brought it back to have a play
Well, that is my theory
I know it's weak at best
But just in case I've got it wrong
I've got the cats some chicken breast

CLUMSY

Although you may think I'm all together
I'm the accident-prone type
And I wish that I could have
A few less bruises in my life
I know my eyesight's rubbish
But it started way before that
Looking back, I realised
I've always been a clumsy twat
I've a gift for falling down and tripping up
Of flying over the handlebars on my bike
Our simply tumbling down a hillside
Whilst out on a gentle hike
But my finest moment ever
Was getting dressed for a posh do
A chain of events I couldn't
Recreate if I tried to
I had a silky dress on
And these snazzy vintage boots
I was looking pretty good
And had a fancy hat to suit
But this is where it all went wrong
While fiddling with my hat and hair
My boot laces got entangled
Right at the top of the stairs
I tried to step forward to regain my balance
But I got such a fright
As I couldn't step to safety
As my dress was just too tight
With my hat over my eyes
And my laces in a knot
A reached out to stop me falling
Down the stairs but I forgot

That the door frame I grabbed hold of
Opened out the other way
And I crushed my little fingers
And said some words you shouldn't say
So, the day didn't turn out
The way I wanted it to be
But I was the fanciest dressed woman
Down at the local A & E

LITTLE BAT

Little tiny bat flying round the arena
Were you aware that we'd all seen ya?
We were waiting for the hockey game to start
When all of a sudden you came flying aht
You dove and swooped across the ice
We all went, awww cos you're small and nice
Perhaps you were searching for the puck
Or just fancied a closer look?
I'd have liked you to come and sit with me
Or even better do a doodoo on the referee
I would have given you a nibble of my hot dog
If you'd have landed on his head to drop a log
Oh the things you must have seen
Up close and personal with the team
If I were you, I'd swoop and zoom
Right into the changing room
I wonder, do you live in there?
Flying around without a care
When we've all gone home do you pinch the snacks?
When the lights are off, and it's pitch black?
Then it's time to come out and eat the grub
Perhaps a little beer in your little bat pub?
Oh tiny bat you are so sweet
I wish that you could see this tweet
So you'd know how much I care
I really hope next weekend you'll be there

ESTHER PEACHES

This is the story of Esther Peaches
A strange girl with some peculiar features
To look at her you'd never know
As she didn't have them out on show
She had what some call genetic mutations
But no one complained about her aberrations
In fact, Esther regarded them with pride
She had extra nipples, one on each side
Just like when a dog has lots of teats
Esther was blessed with extra treats
It gave our Esther lots of pleasure
And considering what she did for leisure
Meant there was lots of Esther to tweak and rub
When she hung out down the swinger's club
Nobody ever went without you see
Although her tits soon reached her knees
You see all that tweaking had an effect
They stretched a bit although remained erect
But no one cared and neither did she
For she had another anomaly
As well as extra nipples folk also found
Something else next to her lady mound
Esther was such a lucky chick
She had a little lady dick
When God made Esther, it seems to be
She won the genitalia lottery
Esther fortunately swung both ways
Yet could pleasure just herself for days
It seemed there was nothing she couldn't do
And no one she wouldn't do it to
But alas one day she took it too far
And took to dogging in her car

Her assets of what she was quite proud
Soon attracted quite the crowd
The car lights were on, the windows down
Surrounded by all the wankers in the town
They were going for it like you wouldn't believe
Watching Esther and her dogging mate, Spunky Steve
The excitement grew as they put on a show
But unfortunately, when everyone reached the big O
There were too many, the unhappy ending is...
Poor Esther drowned in a sea of jizz

MOJO

Someone stole my mojo
Who it was I don't recall
I must have had one years ago
But now I just feel small
I'm not sure what it does
But I can tell it's not there
Cos I don't feel very groovy
I know there's summat wrong, I swear
I can't be arsed to get out of bed
Or dress nice or do my hair
And I can't be bothered doing stuff
I'm just a lump just sitting there
I've looked in my handbag
But all I found was an old hanky
And a packet of extra strong mints
That have gone soft and a bit manky
I tried down the back of the sofa
That only turned up lots of dust
That shows you how much action that's had
Not the scene of love and lust
Maybe I could order one
I should check online
Even a second hand one I'll settle for
Can you get them on Amazon Prime?
If I had a mojo, I'd be unstoppable
I'd laugh and smile and be full of glee
I'd be off with all the sexy folk
And going to parties
But until I find my mojo
I'll just wait here in the wings
Watching all the others
Do great and wondrous things

I reckon I'll just wait here
A bit rubbish and mojo free
But if you find it wandering about somewhere
Send it back home to me

HEATING

I'm not putting the heating on
You can sit there in your coat
Do you think I'm made of money?
I'm skint, I really haven't owt
My fuel bills are rising
My wages are going the other way
So, I'm afraid you'll have to wear more layers
It's really not that cold today
Yes, I know your hands are freezing
And your fingertips are blue
But it costs a fortune every minute
I'm not fibbing, it's all true
When I was little, we didn't have heating
Our windows had frost on the inside
So, think yourself lucky we haven't now
And see, we all survived
Put some extra socks on
Yes, and on your hands as well
I can't pay the leccy bill
As I've got nowt left to sell
Let us gather round a candle
To keep us warm at night
And if I'm feeling generous
I might even set it alight
If we put a mirror by it
It will seem like we have two
See I'm getting all resourceful
I've got other ideas too
Put the pets on the bed
They might give out some heat
I've got catnip in my socks
So, they will cuddle round my feet

And don't forget my hot flushes
And the heat radiation
Who would have thought being menopausal?
Could improve our situation
There is one other thing
That might raise our body heat
But I'm keeping my woolly jumper on
And the cats are staying on my feet
So, it's up to you to warm us up
Go on go for it full throttle
Go and get the sleeping bags
And I'll fill up the hot water bottle

KEEP MUM

I needed something positive
Something happy in my life
I spend all day being worker, cleaner, mum, cat mum and wife
I get up at daft o'clock
To squeeze in some exercise
To feed the cats and start my work
Before the others even rise
If I'm lucky I might even get
Time for a cup of tea
And if I'm really lucky there's chance
I get an unaccompanied wee
Then after a busy day at work
When some sit down and rest their head
I become shopper, cook and pot washer
And run a taxi service instead
But it's ok cos while I'm waiting
For others to do their fun hobbies
I can crack on with more emails
Or home admin type jobbies
Eventually I'm home again
A quick bath and do some writing
But now they are hungry and need help with homework
While my bed looks so inviting
At last, an hour of me time
I've finally been left alone
Which is where I got this life advice
From someone in my phone
What I need to make me feel good
Is to find a new pastime
Just an hour or two each day
For a new hobby that's just mine

I must say I restrained myself
From saying what was in my head
If I had an extra hour or two
I'd be spending it in bed
I decided to give up
I'd turn the light off and zone out
When "get the bucket, I feel sick"
Was what I heard someone shout
I got out of bed and got it
I can find it in the dark
And I did tummy rubs and medicine
Being a mums a proper lark
Eventually I got back to bed
Where I got about three hours rest
Until the alarm went off again
Then it's time to get up again and dressed
I realised I'd missed something
I'd forgotten hobby time
I'd better start multitasking
I'm sure I'll squeeze it in just fine
I'm sure in that minute in the toilet
I can do a mindfulness class
And perhaps some yoga in the car
Or learn to salsa in the bath
Whilst I'm doing all the ironing
I'll study archaeology
And while I'm being a maths tutor
I'll get an astrophysics PhD
I'm sorry if this sounds sarcastic
And my words not that sincere
It's just us mums are bloody knackered
So, stuff your life advice my dear

UNWANTED GIFT

The unwanted gift
Left under the tree
Or listed on E Bay
Slightly used, yeah that's me
With all that potential
To be all that you need
But it seems my instructions
Were just too hard to read
Perhaps on closer inspection
When taken out of the box
You found me less appealing
Than novelty socks
Thanks for the gift you say
With a convincing smile
Then in the cupboard I go
For a very long while
Occasionally played with
But you're really not keen
I'll turn up at a car boot sale
Good as new, sparkling clean
A proper bargain to be had
Just the box is battered and worn
But then I'll be picked up
And be opened and reborn
Some lucky buyer
Finding a hidden gem
They'll take me home
And I'll be everything to them
The packaging will be taken off
Consigned to the bin
And I'll feel all special
Because I'll matter to him

So don't come crying to me
When you realise that I
Was the gift that you needed
It's too late now goodbye
I don't like waste
I'm recycling you too
Free to good home
Yeah, matey that's you

SERVICE

I think I need a service
A check to see what's wrong with me
If I were a car
I wouldn't pass my MOT
My clutch, I think it's gone
I feel I'm crunching all my gears
And my mileage must be huge
Needs winding back about twenty years
I think I need new brakes
As I just can't seem to stop
Getting into trouble
I've been a few times round the block
If I were in Autotrader
I'd be runner or good for parts
As I've lost my showroom splendour
And my engine doesn't always start
My tyres are flat, my paintwork chipped
And my polish has lost its lustre
And a quick trip down the shop
Is all the adventure I can muster
I'm not like the new snazzy cars on telly
Those all electric shiny visions
I'm ready for the junkyard
And I've got quite high emissions
But don't feel too bad for me
This isn't some sad little sonnet
I'm not a bad old banger
If someone wants to buff my bonnet

WHEELBARROW RACE

In my village many years ago
There was an annual event
That brought us all out to watch
As it was not without incident
A competitive little race
Over two and half miles
Not for the feint hearted
But it didn't half raise some smiles
You entered it in pairs
One to push and one to ride
And needed a wheelbarrow
That one of you sat inside
Better trained than proper athletes
Health and safety? No not here
The only proper skills you needed
Was how to push and hold your beer
You see there was an extra challenge
To stop at each pub along the route
And both down half a pint of beer
There was no booze free substitute
By the time they got near our house
They'd had a little push uphill
And the beers had took effect
So, some would look a little ill
Side to side they would be veering
Red faced and sweaty, we'd cheer and shout
And when they got a wobble on
Their partners would fall out
Now tradition was when you'd done the race
You'd go on a pub crawl all day
So, they probably didn't notice
They'd lost some flesh along the way

And even if they had
The odd bruise or cut
It didn't really matter
So long as you picked your barrow up
If you were proper hard core
You'd ride it home that night
Ah those folks from all those years ago
Knew how to do things right
We haven't got many pubs left now
Everyone's too stiff and straight and narrow
But if you're game let's bring it back
I've got a six pack and a barrow
Let's reintroduce
The wheelbarrow race
But you jump in because I'm pushing
I'm not landing on my face

CLOSE ENCOUNTER

They say you meet folk at the shops
You might even get a date
But I got more than I expected
And not a potential mate
I nipped in for some biscuits
And something nice for tea
When some drunken fella in a state
Got way too close to me
I checked out my suitor's basket
Were we compatible in our tastes?
But he only had a bag of flour
And smelled a bit like human waste
He leaned across the conveyor belt
And tried to touch my goods
So, I told him most politely
To go away, no thank you bud
But he didn't get the message
And then he leaned on me
I really got a lungful
Of his perfume, eau de wee
I pulled back in horror
Gave a glare and disapproving tut
Then he swung around quite wildly
And then stepped back on my foot
I threw my money at the checkout girl
And left as swiftly as I could
I didn't reckon I had a future
With my supermarket stud
If he's the best that I can do
I'm giving up on life
Maybe I'm shopping in the wrong places
Or should just find me a wife

So next week I've ordered my stuff online
I'm not going back there again
Instead, I'm going down the bookshop
To see if they've got better men
Well, they might not be much better
But at least I'll know they can read
And at least the customers in there
Don't smell like dog shit, piss and weed

INDICATORS

Please use your indicators
Those blinky little things
Because it's kind of helpful
To know where you're going
Is it safe to overtake you?
Have you stopped? Will you pull out?
I don't know what you're doing
Yet you seem angry when I shout
I'm afraid I'm not clairvoyant
My psychic powers below par
So, I really don't know what the hell
You are doing in your car
You seem to have pulled up
In the middle of the road
Is there some blockage up in front?
Or have you just stopped to unload?
If I dare to try and pass you
On the school run this fine morning
Will you take my passenger door off?
When you set off without warning?
I know you're extra special
By the flash car that you drive
But the rest of us mere mortals
Just want to stay alive
So, when you are sat there in your Audi
BMW or 4X4
Just look down a bit and remember
Us peasants being scraped up off the floor
Please do us all a favour
And follow the highway code
Or do us an even bigger one
And just keep off the road

I'm not saying that I'm perfect
I might bend the rules a bit
But at least folk know what I'm doing
Unlike you, who is just a tit

IT'S GONE

For those that do not know
That dreaded covid bug found me
And today I got a big surprise
When giving the cats their tea
I chose a lovely meaty offering
I gave the packet a little rip
And awaited that lovely moment
When the whiff would make me gip
But what's this, it wasn't there
No horrible stench to offend my nose
So, I went to the washing basket
And stuck my face in the dirty clothes
This can't be right I muttered
With arms full of sweaty gym gear
I can't smell a single thing
There's something not working here
I'd heard covid stops you smelling smells
Perhaps it's that I'll do more tests
I checked the cat litter and my husband
Which put the case to rest
If I can't smell him not in the slightest
Then my senses have truly departed
As he generally gives something off
Like rotten meat, or he's just farted
So alas I cannot detect a thing
Which makes the risks a little higher
As my cooking is bad enough already
How will I know if it's on fire?
I haven't eaten yet either
So not sure if my taste's gone too
But that might be a welcome relief
As my food often takes like poo

Perhaps this will be just what I need
To shed that extra fat
I can eat celery instead of chocolate
I could end up thin as a lat
So, I'm in no rush to get it back
It really doesn't seem like hell
Keep an eye out for the slim new me
Just tell me if I smell

HAPPY

I should be happy
I should have fun
I should have someone to bite my bum
But I just have two cats and a bottle of rum
It sucks being me
I want to smile
I want to swoon
I want to be shagged senseless in every room
But I've just got face ache, the bringer of doom
It sucks being me
I need to giggle
I need to sigh
I need to be that twinkle in someone's eye
I need a good seeing to and that's no lie
It sucks being me
I would be cuddly
I would be clean
I would do things that were slightly obscene
I would even be your bondage queen
It sucks being me
I could be sexy
I could be a tease
I could have carpet burns on my knees
I could even do weird stuff with cheese
It sucks being me
But I don't have any
I don't have a laugh
I've got a dodgy knee and a big overdraft
And I'm always knackered from too much graft
It sucks being me
So, If you're a half decent fella
Come take me away

You just need to be normal
And not secretly gay
Come on, I'm waiting day after day
Come rescue me

BUMBLE BEE

Little bumble bee
Lying there upon the floor
You're looking pretty knackered
Like you just can't fly no more
Would you like a cup of tea
Or perhaps want me to stroke your head
You're not moving all that much
I really hope that you're not dead
You don't seem all that safe
On the pavement where you lie
So, I'm going to put you somewhere else
Until you've got the strength to fly
Please don't be scared while I move you
I'll be gentle as can be
I'm going to put you in my garden
So, you can be safe with me
I've got lots of lovely flowers
Like an all you can eat buffet
So even when you get your energy back
I'd really like it if you'd stay
So little bee in my garden
Once you're feeling on the mend
Feel free to bumble round some more
And be my little fuzzy friend

WHITE NOISE

You're here in every meeting, we all hear your point of view
But the problem is we never hear anyone but you
You talk over all the others as they try to interject
I think your parents never taught you much about respect
Your ego is enormous, of course you're always right
Well in your opinion, but we all think that you talk shite
When I hear your voice all I hear is blah blah blah
You are the most irritating person in my life...so far
You've done everything, been everywhere, you tell us what will and what won't work
And yet you never produce anything, you pompous little jerk
You're just talking bollocks, you are white noise in the room
Come on let's see some actions, while I picture you meeting your doom
I'm not even listening to you now
Just sketching you with an axe in your head
And as for the fella next to me
He's listing ways to make you dead
So, I think it's time you canned it
Take a hint, get a new job
Cos no one really likes
A self important knob

POOR JACK

This is a tale of caution
All you fellas heed this tale
About poor Jack and an event
That made him turn quite pale
He'd always been a wanker
This part of the story is no shock
But one day he fiddled with himself so much
He just pulled off his cock
His mates were in denial, in disbelief
Others cringed a bit and shivered
But it's true he drained himself of jus
So, his old chap was dry and withered
His mum she'd always warned him
She made him mittens to wear for bed
So, he couldn't do things in the darkness
But he did it all day instead
At every opportunity he'd play with himself
Even watching Lorraine on daytime telly
Who would have thought that big Jack jacking off?
Would leave little Jack shrivelled on his belly
It really was a shock to the nurses
When he went to get it fixed
That compared to the size of his biceps
He had a tiny twiglet dick
They tried to sew the thing back on
But I'm afraid it couldn't be
He'd put a lifetime's wear and tear
Into his small lifeless pee pee
So, you chaps just take it steady
Let Jack's mishap be a warning
Stick with homes under the hammer
DO NOT watch Holly on This Morning

GIFT

Because I like you, I wanted to give a gift only for you
But I'm skint and can't afford to so this poem will have to do
I could bake you a cake full of love you lucky fella
And I'd try really really hard not to give you salmonella
I could make you a picture, a masterpiece no doubt
But I can't think what to draw and my felt tips have all run out
Perhaps to flout convention I could pick you a bunch of flowers
Or maybe we could just stay in, and you know what for a few hours
I could take you on a day out and even buy you an ice cream
Or we could do something naughty but I'm really trying to keep this clean
There are so many things that I could think of
Ways to make you smile
A gift doesn't seem enough
As they only last for a short while
So, take this poetic offering
For words are all I've got
But if I win the lottery
Then I'll get you the whole damn lot

I'M HUNGRY

I'm feeling very hungry
Cos I've started on this diet
I've got to shift some fat
But don't tell anyone I'm keeping it quiet
I've worked out all of my meals
They're all balanced and nutritious
But fruit and veg and chuffing rice cakes
Are not what I would call delicious
The problem is I've got a sweet tooth
It's a hard addiction to break
I'm a proper sugar junkie
And I really want some cake
But I won't cos I'm a good girl
I won't give in, but I might grumble
Why does there have to be
Half a million calories in apple crumble
I've drunk gallons of water
To feel less hungry or so they say
But I'm still starving
And I've been to the toilet twenty times today
We're completely out of loo roll
People think I've got the shits
I might swap the water for a G&Tt
That might slow the flow a bit
I've chewed the top off of my biro
I've even sniffed the biscuit tin
Why is it so bloody hard?
I only want to be nice and thin
But I am going to get there
Cos my trousers don't look right
And I'm not buying new ones
I'm from Yorkshire I'm too tight

But I'll just issue this warning
Don't eat anywhere near me
Because I'm not thinking straight
I've only had salad for tea
I might nick your spicy noodles
Or just grab your sausage bap
And don't be surprised if I just snatch
Your scotch eggs from your lap
I don't think I can be trusted
Around food I've no control
I never could resist something to suck
Or say no to a swiss roll
So, I've warned you I'm dead hungry
Be nice to me or I may bite
As I'm feeling awfully grumpy
Cos this diet malarkey is shite

PET SHOP

I visited a pet shop
Like no other I have seen
An outlet stocked with body parts
It felt like a bad dream
I'm used to cat food and dog biscuits
Pet toys and baskets those kind of things
Not random limbs of animals
With stuff horns and goosey wings
Seriously what kind of lunatic
Gives their dog this stuff as a treat
What's wrong with good old Bonio
Not severed ears or chicken feet
What are they trying to do to folk?
Do they really want your kids to see
Fluffy the little poodle
Chewing on something's knee
Where does it all come from anyway
Is there a special farm to rear these things?
Ill-fated little creatures
All with missing ears and limbs
I've never seen for sale before
A pile of bunny ears with fur still on
Six for a pound it said, a snip
Well, it was for the wabbit cos his lugs are gone
It did give me an idea though
For later on this year
To send my kid out in Halloween fancy dress
Guaranteed to cause maximum fear
I'll dress her as Maleficent
With beef stuffed horns upon her head
And a bucket for of rabbit ears
And some chewy hooves to knock em dead

I'll glue them on her shoes
Some little trotters on her feet
My offal cladded child is bound
To clean up trick or treat
But while this moment comes
And it's the scary time of year
I'll go scouring the countryside
To find these rabbits with no ears

THE LITTLE FART THAT WASN'T

This poem is not a long one
But there is a tale to tell
About Steven and the incident
That left a funny smell
He was acting a little reckless
Trying to make a funny clip
About his farting prowess
So, he filmed himself let rip
But there was a lack of judgement
He hadn't thought it through
He'd had coffee and bran muffins
But not his morning poo
He lined the camera up
He lunged and then he flexed
He even went and got changed
Into a brand new pair of kecks
Some people, they may mock him
They may say he had it coming
When he let one go and then below
He sensed something was running
Poor Steven he had blundered
Poor Steven was a tit
But his tweet went bloody viral
As he farted out a shit

POUND SHOP PRINCESS

The fashion guru
The queen of style
Watch her strutting down the aisle
With green plastic nails
And patchy tan
She's out to get herself a man
Her hair scraped up in a donut bun
And a g string lodged right up her bum
Her make up is a work of art
With drawn on brows she looks the part
A seductress for the hard of sight
She'll drag anyone into her lair for the night
The pound shop princess is on the prowl
With her foundation slapped on with a trowel
Look out fellas she is intent
To lure you in with her one-pound scent
A fragrance made from coconut and peach
With undertones of gin and bleach
She's all set up for slap and tickle
She's bought pound lube, johnnies and peanut brittle
Well, you need the nuts for energy
Cos she's one demanding lady
But don't worry if you need help to shag her
She's got a stash of pound Viagra
The princess of glitter gloss and sparkle
With way more class than that Miss Markle
A catch for those with a strong yearning
For love who don't mind their wee wee burning
With pound champagne
And pound lingerie
She's the cheapest date there could ever be
So, the pound shop princess is ready and waiting

If you're ready for some discount dating

MISS HOME BARGAINS 2022

I met a delightful woman the other day
Miss home bargains 2022
A little on the aggressive side
I think she had a few other issues too
I was quietly perusing the products
In search of freezer bags
When my view was repeatedly blocked
By this domineering hag
She seemed to be on a mission
To put her vast bottom in my way
And whichever way I turned
She waddled over the same way
There appeared some real intent
She wouldn't leave me alone
But I didn't know how I was angering
The grumpy frowning crone
So, to make her feel included
My space invading dragon
I revved her up by asking
For some help with my bagging
Her stubby tattooed fingers clenched
I could feel her ill will
As she hurled my battered shopping
Towards my bags across the till
But I had another trick
To increase her aggravation
I paid for my shopping
In very small denominations
A fistful of shrapnel
I thrust in her bloated hand
And bid her a good day
Which left me feeling rather grand

WHEN I AM GONE

When I am gone
And I am no more
Just leave me in a bin bag
Outside the door
I don't need tears
Or sad goodbyes
Or people saying I was nice
Or other lies
Just raise a glass to me
Down the pub
Get pissed on gin
Then go out for grub
I don't want fancy flowers
It's a waste of money
And they'll only get nicked
Or go all brown and funny
Take my stuff down the charity shop
My books are shite
So, in the bin they'll pop
I ain't got money
So don't wait for the will
And anyroad you probably didn't visit
When I was ill
I never had owt
So there's no inheritance
So I don't mind if you just
Say good riddance
I never liked folk anyway
So I won't mind if I'm just thrown away
Or donate my bits to medical science
Give them trainee doctors a good laugh

It's got to be better for your back
Than dragging the bin bag down the path
I didn't achieve much with my life
So just send me on my way
But check with the local council first
You get the right bin collection day
You could leave me in garden
Let the birds peck at my ass
But I'll probably smell a bit fruity
And cause a yellow patch on the grass

OTHER BOOKS BY THE AUTHOR

Modern Times & Hard Rhymes by poet Laura J. Booker covers the ups and downs of modern life, in her own unique acid tongue, comic verse kind of way.

Warning this is for adults only Laura J. Booker tells how it is the hard way.
So, if you are easily offended you best just go away.

She's like a modern-day Pam Ayres, but with a lot more bite!

AMAZON UK:
https://amzn.to/3CmfGoq

AMAZON USA:
https://amzn.to/3Ci7vJL

SHOOTING FROM THE LIP

Shooting From the Lip by Laura J. Booker is the second collection of her hilarious and wonderfully edgy poems.
She doesn't shy away from delicate subjects, has always a strong opinion.
So, if you are easily offended, we do not recommend Laura J. Booker for you.
But if you like a right good laugh and having this crazy world flipped on its head and the pompous and arrogant put in their place, she's the lady for you.

She's from Yorkshire after all and Laura always "Shoots from the lip!"

We do have to warn you this book contains adult themes:

AMAZON UK:
https://amzn.to/3Nk3iel

AMAZON USA:
https://amzn.to/3wAZMGD

ABOUT THE AUTHOR

Laura J Booker is a wife, mother, and obedient servant to her two cats. Born and bred in South Yorkshire Laura says it as it is, she began writing poetry during the first covid lockdown as a way to deal with the stress and find humour in those strange times, she continues to find strange things everywhere.

Her first poetry collection *Modern Times & Hard Rhymes* was a resounding success and amazingly wasn't banned. Her second outing *Shooting from the Lip* was an even bigger success.
This third volume *Drawing A Blank*, might very well be the best yet.
Drawing a Blank, is the third in the trilogy and we can but hope that more poems and verse will soon flow from her pen.

Printed in Great Britain
by Amazon